VIKING
CAPITAL RAISING

Chapter 1:

Bank Loans

Every business starts with a small team and a great idea, but not always extensive business experience. If you previously worked in a different industry or haven't worked in a small business before, you face a steep learning curve in order to bring your idea to life. Starting a business means finding staff, premises, suppliers, and so many other things that can only be secured with capital. In this book, you'll learn about the most popular options small businesses can use to raise capital and begin their work. Chapter one will look at loans, chapter two will look at investment opportunities, and chapter three will look at how you can raise capital from within your community. Let's start off by looking at the kinds of loans a small business can secure.

Bank Loans

This might be the first option you consider when it comes to securing capital, particularly if you don't have much small business experience. It's a logical step, given that bank loans often have the lowest interest rates. The two most common types of business bank loans are fixed and flexible. Fixed loans have pre-determined payment schedules and interest rates, whereas with flexible loans, these factors are decided according to your business and financial needs. Fixed loans tend to have more widespread repayment schedules, and with either type of loan, the repayment term can be between one and fifteen years, depending on the loan amount. Interest rates on business bank loans tend to be between seven and twelve per cent, though this figure will depend on a variety of factors such as the loan amount and the financial climate.

However, it's often very difficult for new and small businesses to secure bank loans. Many banks have drastically reduced their small business loan approval rate, citing the high risk of failure as the reason. In order to qualify for a bank loan, your company will need great credit, revenue, profitability, cashflow and experience- if you have all that, you probably don't need a start-up loan. A good example of this situation is securing your loan. A secured loan requires you to offer "security"- an asset that the bank can seize if your company fails to repay as planned. Secured loans offer larger amounts and lower interest rates, but loans can only be secured by companies with property or substantial assets. In reality, bank loans are a rare choice for small businesses.

SBA Loans

The SBA (Small Business Administration) is an independent agency of the U.S. government that offers a variety of services to small businesses. It does not offer loans, but works with commercial lending partners to offer loans to public and private organizations. The SBA vets its lenders and all loans must follow its requirements, making the process less risky for borrowers and lenders. SBA loans are only available to U.S. companies that do not have reasonable access to other funding opportunities. The SBA offers four kinds of loans;

general small business loans, microloans, real estate and equipment loans, and disaster loans. Each of these loans have specific uses and when applying for them, you must show what you plan to do with the money.

A general small business loan general small business loan is the most common type of SBA loan and has the widest range of uses. It falls into the 7(a) category of SBA loans and its uses include purchasing commercial property or equipment, paying for operational expenses, and refinancing debt. Businesses are eligible to apply for this loan if their net worth does not exceed $15 million or they have an average net income greater than $5 million over the last two years. The maximum amount that can be borrowed is $5 million and there is no minimum amount. Interest rates are negotiated by the SBA and the lending partner.

A microloan is typically used to start or expand a new business, and it cannot be used to repay debt or purchase real estate. Interest rates for these loans tend to be between 8 and 13% with a maximum repayment term of six years.

A real estate and equipment loan, as the name suggests, can be used to purchase real estate or equipment. It can also be used to fund the construction, conversion, or renovation of existing commercial property. In order to qualify for this loan your company must be on the SBA's list of eligible businesses, not have funds available from any other sources, and not be engaged or planning to engage in rental real estate investment.

A disaster loan is a low-interest loan provided to repair or replace items that have been damaged or destroyed in a declared natural disaster. Such items include real estate, business assets, personal property, machinery, equipment, and inventory.

Chapter 2:
Investors

Securing investment as a small business can simultaneously seem like it will be incredibly easy and incredibly difficult. Investors are individuals you can appeal to and impress with your great idea, rather than giant faceless banks. However, investors often have less money to spare than larger institutions. The best way to clinch investors is to know how they work- luckily for you, that's exactly what you're about to learn.

Venture Capitalists

A venture capitalist can be an individual, but it is usually a professionally-managed firm that invests other people's money on their behalf. Venture capital firms pool money from a range of investors and invest in small companies that can prove they will provide a high return. Venture capitalists are not interested in companies that want to work on a small scale- they're looking to get in on the ground floor with companies that will grow to be industry titans. Investing in a small business is risky, so venture capitalists expect a high return, equity in the company, access to financial records and a say in large decisions. From their perspective, these things are required to make the investment worth their while.

Due to their extensive professional experience, some small businesses bring venture capitalists on board for their advice as well as their investments. However, it can be a poor choice for those who want to maintain control of their business. The best way to grab the attention of a venture capitalist is to be referred to them by a financial professional, such as a banker or accountant.

Angel Investors

Where a venture capitalist invests someone else's money, an angel investor uses their own. Angel investing has soared in popularity in recent years, as individuals have better access to educational resources and discover new alternatives to traditional financial options like savings accounts. Most angel investors are not incredibly wealthy. This might seem like a downside as they have less money to invest, but the upside is that you probably already know a lot of angel investors. Angel investors might be current or former colleagues, entrepreneurs, or people in your social circle who invest in their spare time. Another significant difference between venture capitalists and angel investors is that angels aren't entirely motivated by profit. They are more likely to be inspired by a great pitch and back a company because they want to see it succeed, rather than simply because they think they'll get a high return. Angel investors typically expect less control in the company than venture capitalists, instead looking for a share in the company they believe will be successful one day.

Angel investors can be divided into two categories: affiliated and non-affiliated. Affiliated angels are people you already know, that you can reach out to through an appointment or personal meeting. Non-affiliated angels are people that have no connection to you or your business. The best ways to find non-affiliated angels include advertising in business papers, working with business brokers or intermediaries, and simply spreading the word through your social circles. If you already know some angels, they will probably be able to introduce you to even more potential investors.

Chapter 3:

Alternatives

When you have a business idea, your friends and family are going to be the first ones to know about it. They'll have spent months, or maybe even years, listen to you talk about your plans and watch you build your business from the ground up. Those closest to you may want to support your dreams, but it's important to find the balance between professional and personal. You want your business to succeed, but that doesn't mean sacrificing close relationships. In this chapter, you'll find a few tips for encouraging capital in a healthy and safe way.

Gifts

Particularly when you're starting up, generous friends or relatives may offer you a small cash gift to help with those first few expenses. This can be great, as long as it's definitely a gift and not actually a loan. If your company becomes financially successful, you might find that people you believed were giving you gifts now expect their money to be repaid. The best way to avoid this is to clearly communicate to the other person that this is a gift when you receive the money- a step up from this is to have that communication in writing. It might be awkward, but it's a key part of keeping things professional.

Loans

Friends and family members are less likely to charge you interest than any other financial source, so this can be a great way to raise money without added expenses. However, these loans will probably be smaller than those from banks or investors, and your personal spending may be under scrutiny while you're in debt to this other person. It's best to work with a business attorney or a peer-to-peer lending company so everything is above board and professional.

Equity

If you have friends or relatives who believe in your company's mission, they may want to be a part of it. Like selling an equity to an investor, this will not work for people who want to retain full control of their company. It's also important to consider how working with this person as a business partner will affect your personal relationship. If you decide to sell equity to this person, make sure to involve a business attorney so everything is official.

Crowdfunding

Crowdfunding has gained popularity in recent years, with sites like Kickstarter and IndieGoGo allowing billions of dollars to be raised by small businesses. When you crowdfund, your plan for the raised money is clearly visible to backers so they know exactly what's happening when they donate. You can use rewards-based crowdfunding and give your backers unique rewards in exchange for their donations, or use equity-based crowdfunding and sell small parts of the company. However,you do it, the process is formalized through the crowdfunding platform and it's clear that the money donated will not be repaid. If you're unsure about involving friends and family through other methods, crowdfunding might be the best option for you.

Conclusion

When you start a new business, the dreams of success can sometimes feel weighed down by the reality of financial planning. Maybe this company will bring you millions one day, but right now you need to focus on that first boost that will help you get started. The three main ways you can raise capital are loans, investors, and friends and family. Bank loans can be difficult to secure as a small business, but there are groups like the SBA specifically designed for companies that are ineligible for traditional funding avenues.

When it comes to investors, the size and goals of your business may determine whether you should aim for a venture capitalist or an angel investor. If you decide to involve your friends and family in your company's finances, make sure to treat it like a business decision so there are no blurred lines between personal and professional. Within each financial avenue, you'll have a series of choices based on what suits your business best. After all, it's your business and it's important to do what works for you.

www.ingramcontent.com/pod-product-compliance
Lightning Source LLC
Chambersburg PA
CBHW040931210326

41597CB00030B/5268